MW00957356

Cricut Tips the Ultimate Troubleshooting Guide

How to Master Your Cricut Machine

Maryann Gillespie

ISBN-13:978-1496188274
ISBN-10:1496188276

Copyright © 2014 All rights reserved.

This book is for your personally enjoyment only.
No part of this book may be copied, distributed or
reproduced in any form without written permission
from the author.

Table of Contents

Introduction 4

Chapter One - Cricut Machines and Troubleshooting Techniques.. 8

Chapter Two - Help With Cricut Cartridges 24

Chapter Three - Ending the Blade Blues 33

Chapter Four - Cutting Mat Miracles 40

Chapter Five - Working With Gel Pens and Markers... 47

Chapter Six - Used Cricuts the Good the Bad and the Ugly 50

Chapter Seven - Favorite Adhesives Paper and Tools.. 53

Chapter Eight - Money Saving Tricks.......................... 59

Chapter Nine - Conquering Craft Room Chaos............ 65

Chapter Ten - Turning Ordinary Days into Special Occasions... 69

Chapter Eleven - Warranty Warning............................ 72

Chapter Twelve - DIY Repairs and Resources............. 73

Chapter Thirteen - How to Video Tutorials.................. 77

Chapter Fourteen - FAQs 81

Chapter Fifteen - Your Opinion Matters 87

About The Author... 88

Introduction

My name is Maryann Gillespie and I love my Cricut. I couldn't always say this, though. For the first several weeks I fought with my machine and spouted some very unpleasant words in its direction. I was tempted to box it up and put it in the closet along with a few other craft machines I've purchased through the years.

But then I started to learn a few tricks. These slight tweaks changed my experience form frustrated to pleasurable.

I've been a crafter for several years. I slaved over intricate baby books for my children. I became a crafter on steroids making sure everyone in the family got tons of cute, artsy-fartsy creations.

One of the breakthroughs in my crafting expertise was purchasing my Cricut machine. Once I mastered it the possibilities were endless.

I currently use the Cricut Expression and I'm thrilled with everything it does. Not only do I use it for my scrapbooking but for a host of other crafting projects.

I don't even remember the last time I purchased a greeting card. I could never be happy with boxes of store bought cards again.

A few of my favorite projects include using vinyl to make wall art, and personalizing my kid's toys and practically everything else in their rooms. I'm sure you have a long list of your favorite Cricut project ideas too.

The Cricut can be used to cut paper, vinyl, fabric and a bunch of other stuff. You can cut letters from an assortment of fonts as well as thousands of graphic images. You're truly only limited by your imagination.

You'll find yourself walking through department stores looking at expensive decorative pieces and thinking "I can make that at home using my Cricut".

If you ever need inspiration for new crafts projects just go to Pinterest and view the projects others have posted. Looking through these will get your own creativity juices flowing into high gear.

I love my Cricut because it allows me to use my creativity in so many different ways.

However, I've talked to many other women who are still unhappy with their machines. They've never gotten past the annoyed phase.

They become frustrated when their machine messes up or doesn't work properly. So they pack it back into the box and stuff it in the closet. I hate to see that happen.

Not only have these folks spent their hard earned money on an unused machine - but I hate to see the potential of these machines being wasted. I know these crafters would love what they create with their Cricut if they could just master a few tricks and techniques.

I want to help others learn to enjoy their Cricuts as much as I do. It was this desire to help others that inspired this book.

I am not a high-tech person. I'm only telling you that so you'll know if I can learn to use a Cricut so can you. I didn't start with any special knowledge or skills, just the desire to create wonderful art work that could be shared with my family and friends. I have even sold items at craft fairs and farmer's markets.

My hope in writing this book is to help you enjoy your machine and to kiss the frustration good-bye!

Here are a few of the things we'll be learning about in this book:

The pros and cons of the different Cricut machines

How to choose which Cricut to purchase based on your needs

Finding the proper settings for specific materials

How to troubleshoot problems you encounter with your machine

Do the risks outweigh the benefits of buying used Cricut products?

Ways to save money on supplies

Do it yourself repairs

and a host of other ideas, tips and troubleshooting techniques to help you conquer your machine. By the time you finish reading this Cricut book for dummies, you'll be using your die cutter for an assortment of projects.

My goal is to help you learn from some of my mistakes so you can save yourself a lot of time and money. You'll also make some amazing artwork along the way.

Let's get started.

Chapter One - Cricut Machines and Troubleshooting Techniques

I want to start by explaining the differences in the most popular Cricut machines. If you haven't yet bought your Cricut it might help you decide which model you need.

They each have their pros and cons so I can't tell you one is definitely better than the other. They have various capabilities and different price points.

Cricut Personal, Create and Expression

These machines do not require a computer to work. They have their own LCD screen display and keyboard. The designs are programmed using cartridges. If you want to be able to use your machine without connecting to a computer then this is a good option. Each cartridge contains around 700 images so you get a multitude of options with each one.

The Personal and Create machine cuts designs from 1 inch to 5 1/2 inches. (Make sure to read the Warranty Warning chapter to see which machines have been discontinued as this may influence your buying decision)

The Expression machine can cut designs from 1/4 inch to 23 1/2 inches in size. You are able to orient the paper for landscape or portrait.

Usually one font cartridge and one shapes cartridge comes with your machine.

Sometimes you can purchase a bundle with your machine that includes several cartridges at a discounted cost. There's also a chapter later in this book where I tell you about several ways to save on cartridges. You can often find them much cheaper if you know where to look.

These are older machines and you can buy one used on Amazon or eBay if you want to save some money. I discuss the pros and cons of buying used machines in a later chapter.

Cricut Expression 2 Tricks

Version 2 is the newest model of the Expression machine, which is probably the most popular model among Cricuter's. You do not need a computer to use this machine. It has its own screen and keyboard so you program your cuts without ever connecting to a computer.

However, when I'm going to be working on my Cricut for a while I find working with the larger computer screen much more pleasant than the small LCD display. To work on the computer you'll be using the Cricut Craft Room software by Provo Craft - the company that sells Cricuts. All the machines are compatible with the Craft Room, so to get the most functionality from the design software your need to download it and install it on your computer.

An advantage of the Expression 2 is that you don't need the keyboard overlays that were necessary with previous machines. You can see the images on the LCD screen.

This machine allows for a choice of portrait or landscape orientation. Design sizes can be as small as 1/4 inches and as large as 23 1/2 inches. A complaint I often hear is that the machine only comes with a 12 x 12 mat. It seems that if it does the larger cuts it should come with a 12 x 24 inch mat also. But it must be purchased separately.

Cricut Mini Hints

This machine represents a big change from the machines we just discussed. The biggest difference is this one requires being connected to a computer, Windows or Mac and an Internet connection. You can't use it without being connected to your computer and the Cricut Craft Room software.

Because it doesn't have its own built in display or keyboard it is much cheaper to purchase. This makes it a good option for someone who doesn't craft a lot or who wants to test the Cricut waters before making a larger investment.

Also, it is much smaller in size than the other machines. If you like to take your Cricut to crops or to fairs it can be a good choice. But don't forget, you will need to take a laptop, too.

It will take up less room in your house which is handy for those who don't have a dedicated craft space.

The mini will cut paper 8 1/2 by 12. This means the designs it cuts are from 1/4 inch to 11 1/2 inches. It will not cut large designs like the larger machines.

All cartridges are compatible with the Mini except for Imagine cartridges. This little bug even works with the Cricut Gypsy which is the portable hand held design studio.

Troubleshooting Techniques

I realize that no one wants to hear what I'm about to say; but it's important to mention it anyway. When you first get your machine, take some time and look through the user manual.

I know that the Cricut user manuals are not the best in the world. But at least follow the set-up guide carefully. Then look at the chapter on Basic Operations. After that you can refer to the manual as the need requires. When you try something new then at least see what the manual has to say.

The keyboard and commands on the Cricut can seem overwhelming at first. You need to at least familiarize yourself with all the basic commands and icons. You can refer back to the manual later when you need to learn about a specific item.

The least you'll need to know is where to find the speed dial, pressure settings, blade depth, and load mat button.

The guide will walk you through calibrating your machine in the beginning to make sure it's lined up correctly.

Then you'll be given a test project to make your first cut. Follow the directions carefully. Enter each command slowly; the machine can freeze if you give it too many directions too quickly.

Also, read about your warranty. You need to know what your warranty covers, how long it lasts, and what will **void the warranty**. You don't want to do something accidently that will prevent you from returning a machine that is broken and still under warranty.

This next section deals with some of the most common problems I hear users complain about. A lot of these trouble shooting techniques will work on multiple machines, others are machine specific.

Material Tearing or Not Cutting Completely Through

This is the biggest problem with most Cricut users. When this happens the image is ruined and you've wasted material. More machines have been returned or boxed up and put away due to this problem than any other.

But don't panic, if your paper is not cutting correctly there are several steps you can take to try and correct the problem: (the problem could be a blade problem which we discuss in more detail in a later chapter. But I'll touch on a few things briefly in this section. Most important is this: Anytime you work with the blade TURN YOUR MACHINE OFF. I know it's easy to forget this because you're frustrated and you're trying this and that to make it work correctly. But this is an important safety precaution that you should remember. And yes, I'll mention this again in the chapter dedicated to blades!)

Make simple adjustments at first. Turn the pressure down one. Did it help? If not, turn the blade down one number. Also make sure the mat is free of debris so the blade rides smoothly.

Usually the thicker the material, the higher the pressure number should be set to cut through the paper. Don't forget to use the multi cut function if you have that option. It may take a little longer to cut 2, 3 or 4 times, but by then it should cut clean through.

For those of you using the smaller bugs that do not have that option here is how to **make your own multi cut function**. After the image has been cut don't unload the mat just hit load paper, repeat last and cut. You can repeat this sequence 2, 3 or 4 times to ensure your image is completely cut out.

If you are using thinner paper and it is tearing try reducing the pressure and slowing down the speed. When cutting intricate designs you have to give the blade enough time to maneuver through the design by slowing it down it will be able to make cleaner cuts.

Another thing to consider when working with fancy cuts is if you've chosen to cut the design too small, you may have a hard time cutting it out, try increasing the size and see if that helps.

Clean the edge of the blade to be sure no fuzz or scraps of paper are stuck to it.

Make sure the blade is installed correctly. Take it out and put it back so it's seats firmly. The blade should be steady while it's making cuts. If it makes a shaky movement it's either not installed correctly or there's a problem with the blade housing. (To watch how to change blades see the video tutorial section.)

While the blade is out, make sure the housing is clear of any fuzz or debris. Take a piece of wire and clean out the hole in the blade housing or just blow in the hole to get rid of any fibers that collects in the housing. A little routine maintenance can go a long way in preventing cutting problems. When you change the blade make it a habit to clean out the housing.

Switch to a new blade. The problem may be as simple as a dull blade. If the blade is new it could be a **defective blade**. I make recommendations about sharp, long lasting carbon blades in another chapter.

Be aware that there is a deep cutting blade for thicker material. You'll want to switch to this blade when you're cutting heavy card stock. This will also save wear and tear on your regular blade. Cutting a lot of thick material will obviously wear your blade out quicker than thinner material.

Occasionally the problem can be the paper itself. If you've bought cheap paper you might try the same cut with a higher quality paper and see what happens. Also, some card stock has a high fiber content that simply makes clean cuts impossible. If you run into this problem be sure and make note of where you purchased the product and the brand name. You don't want to make the same mistake again. Really thin paper can also be a problem. You may need to tape the paper to the edges of the mat to keep it from slipping around during the cut. If the paper moves while it is being cut it is more likely to rip and tear.

Another big problem is having the settings incorrect for the type of material you're using. This can be confusing; especially when you're just learning the machine or you're working with a new kind of material. I have included a quick cutting chart in the resource section of this book.

Always make sure your mat has enough stickiness to hold the material still while it runs through the machine. We discuss mats in more detail in a later chapter.

Check that the mat has enough clearance as it leaves the machine. If it becomes blocked in any way the mat can be thrown off track.

There are various problems I hear about regarding mats especially involving their stickiness or lack of stickiness. We will discuss these in a later chapter.

Machine Freezing

I've talked to several crafters who say their machines freeze up occasionally.

Remember to always turn your machine off when you switch cartridges. When you switch cartridges leaving the machine on it's called "hot swapping" and it can sometimes cause the machine to freeze. This is more of an issue with the older models and doesn't seem to apply to the Expression 2.

You know how quirky electronic gadgets can be so give your machine a rest for five or ten minutes every hour. If you work for several hours continuously your machine might overheat and freeze up.

Turn the machine off and take a break. Restart it when you come back and it should be fine. Then remember not to rush programming the machine and give it an occasional rest.

Don't press a long list of commands quickly. If you give it too much information too quickly it will get "confused" in the same way a computer sometimes does and simply freeze up. Instead of typing in one long phrase try dividing up your words into several cuts.

If you're using special feature keys make sure you press them first before selecting the letters.

Power Problems

If you turn your machine on and nothing happens the power adapter may be at fault. Jiggle the power cord at the outlet and where it connects to the machine to make sure it's firmly connected. Ideally you want to test the adapter before buying a new one. Swap cords with a friend and see if that fixed the problem. Replacement adapters can be found on eBay by searching for Cricut adapter power supply.

The connection points inside the machine may also pose a problem; here is how to test that. Hold down the plug where it inserts into the back of the machine and turn it on. If it powers up then the problem is inside the machine and the connection points will have to be soldered again.

If the machine powers up but will not cut then try a hard reset. See the resource section for step-by-step instructions on resetting your machine.

Here are a few tips especially for Expression 2 users. Have you turned on your machine, you watch it light up and hear it gearing up but when you try to cut nothing happens or you're stuck on the welcome screen or the LCD screen is unresponsive?

Well here are two quick fixes to try. First try a hard reset sometimes called the rainbow screen reset to recalibrate your die cutter. If that does not resolve the problem you're going to have to restore the settings.

For step-by-step video instructions on resetting and recalibrating your Expression 2 (see the resource section for the link) and watch the video that solves your particular problem.

When using the Cricut Sync software to update your Expression 2 machine, you suddenly get error messages like the device is not recognized or not found, try using a different USB port or temporarily disable your firewall or antivirus software as they may block the updates. Remember to enable them when the updates are complete.

To help cut down on errors try to keep your machine updated. When an update is available you should receive a message encouraging you to install the latest version.

For those of you using third party software that is no longer compatible with the Cricut you probably already know that **updating your machine may disable that software**.

When you cut heavy paper and your Expression 2 shuts down try switching to the normal paper setting and use the multi cut function.

Carriage Will Not Move

If the carriage assembly will not move, check to see if the belt has broken or if the car has fallen off the track. Provo Craft does not sell replacement parts, which is "nuts", so try to find a compatible belt at a vacuum repair shop.

If the wheels have fallen off the track, remove the plastic cover and look for a tiny screw by the wheel unscrew it. You now should be able move the wheel back on track.

Unresponsive Keyboard

If you are sure you are pressing the keys firmly, you have a cartridge inserted correctly and a mat loaded ready to go, but the keypad is still not accepting your selection, the problem may be internal.

You will have to remove the keyboard and check if the display cable is connected to the keypad and to the motherboard. If the connections are secure then you have a circuit board problem and repairs are beyond the scope of this book.

Important reminder, please do not attempt any repairs unless your machine is out of warranty.

Weird LCD Screen

The LCD screen is now showing strange symbols or is blank after doing a firmware update. Try running the update again making sure your selections are correct.

When the image you choose is bigger than the mat or paper size you selected the preview screen will look grayed out instead of showing the image. So increase the paper and mat size or decrease the size of your image.

Also watch out for the gray box effect when using the center point feature. Move the start position down until you see the image appear. The same thing may happen when using the fit to length feature. Try changing to landscape mode and shorten the length size until the image appears.

Occasionally using the undo button will cause the preview screen to turn black; unfortunately the only thing to do is turn the machine off. Your work will be lost and you have to start again.

Cartridge Errors

Sometimes dust or debris accumulates in the cartridge port gently blow out any paper fiber that may have collected in the opening. Make sure the contact points are clean and that nothing is preventing the cartridge from being read properly.

With any electrical machine overheating can be a problem. If you get a cartridge error after using your machine for a while turn it off and let it cool down for about fifteen minutes.

If this is the very first time you're using the cartridge and you get an error I'm sure you know the trick about turning the cartridge around and inserting it in backwards.

I thought I could use my Imagine cartridges with my Expression 2, so why do I get an error message? Because you can only use the art cartridges that you can cut with, the colors and patterns cartridge are for printing.

Even brand-new items fresh out of the box can be defective. If you see a cartridge error 1, 2, 3, 4, 5, 6, 9 or 99 call customer service and tell them the name, serial number and error message number and they may replace the cartridge.

Trouble Connecting to Your Computer

All Cricut machines come with a USB cord that lets you connect to your computer and allows you to use the other products like the Cricut Design Studio software, Cricut Craft Room or the Cricut Gypsy with your machines. (See the Warranty Warning chapter for update information on the DS and Gypsy.)

Double check your USB connection and try another port.

Check to see if you may have a firewall or anti-virus software that is blocking the connection.

See if you're running the latest firmware. You may need to update. Older machines update via firmware (Personal Cutter, Expression, Create and Cake) the newer (Expression 2, Imagine and Gypsy) use the Sync program to update.

When All Else Fails:

I know that no one wants to hear this. But there are going to be times when you may have to resort to calling customer service. This is especially true if your machine is still under warranty. You don't' want to do anything that might void the warranty on a machine that is truly defective.

Sadly, Prove craft is known for its long wait times and sometimes less than stellar service. Stick it out and demand that your machine is fixed or replaced.

Chapter Two - Help With Cricut Cartridges

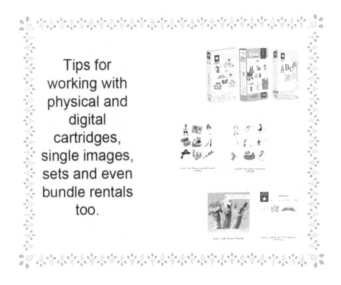

Tips for working with physical and digital cartridges, single images, sets and even bundle rentals too.

Cartridges are an ongoing discussion among Cricut users for a variety of reasons. We will discuss some of those issues in this chapter.

A cartridge is what contains the images and fonts that you'll be cutting. Most cartridges hold 700 or 800 images. Lite cartridges contain about 50 images and have one or two creative features. Despite the limitations you can still be creative and produce hundreds of variations with this less expensive choice.

You usually receive at least one cartridge with the purchase of your machine. Sometimes this is preloaded into your machine as a "digital cartridge".

You may buy downloadable digital cartridges online for immediate use or you can buy the physical plastic cartridges that you slide into your machine.

When you purchase a cartridge; you can use that physical cartridge in your machine or you also have the option to "link" that cartridge to the Cricut Craft Room (CCR).

The Craft Room allows you to view your images on your computer screen which makes it easier to see and manipulate your projects.

By linking to CCR you won't have to bother to physically switch out your cartridges. If you plan to ever sell the cartridges then do NOT link them. Once they are linked you are not legally allowed to sell them. This is understandable. Some people might link them to the craft room so they have access to the images and then sell the physical cartridge.

The complaint that users have is that Provo Craft doesn't provide a way to "unlink" cartridges that you no longer want to use or keep. Hopefully, they will correct this sometime in the future.

To link your cartridges you'll need to do the following. Load the cartridge you want to add into your machine. Go online to the Craft Room. Under all cartridges select my cartridges.You will see a list of cartridges. Find the cartridge you want to add and click "Link" and follow the prompts.

Another advantage to adding your cartridges to the Craft Room is that you'll be able to pull images from several cartridges to use at one time. When you're using the physical cartridge you can only use images from one cartridge at a time.

If you buy a used cartridge you need to ask if it's linked. If it is, you will still be able to use the physical cartridge in your machine but you will not be able to link it to the Craft Room. A cartridge can only be linked once. It is possible to still use the cartridge in the Craft Room but you can't link it. You'll have to have the physical cartridge in your machine to cut the images.

It is now possible to purchase cartridges online and download them to your account. This means you don't have to wait for a physical cartridge to arrive in the mail. You have immediate access to the images. These are the digital cartridges that I referred to earlier.

Many people complain that the cartridges are too expensive. Instead of spending $80 on a cartridge with hundreds of images many people would prefer to be able to buy an image they really want for a dollar or two, that's where single images or sets come in to play.

You can buy single digital images or smaller sets for a fraction of the cost of a full cartridge. You can even rent cartridge bundles for 30 days on the Cricut home page in the shopping section.

Make sure you take advantage of the free cartridges offered in the Craft Room. The only thing to remember is finish your projects. Once the cartridge is no longer free you will not be able to cut your image.

You can save money on cartridges watching for sales and special promotions. We'll talk about ways to save money on cartridges in a later chapter.

It is possible to share physical cartridges with friends. This is good if they want a few images for a special project but don't plan to use the cartridge enough to justify buying it.

At one time you could use third party software to design your own images for use with the Cricut. But Provo Craft has currently made all their machines incompatible with third party software. Users were not happy with this turn of events but so far Provo Craft has not backed down, nor have they provided their own software to make using your own images possible. You can manipulate the cartridge images in many ways to create unique designs. But the images must exist in a cartridge that you own to be able to cut them out.

Digital Handbooks for Easy Reference

Did you know you can download the digital handbook of any cartridge and save it as a PDF file on your computer? Just go to Cricut.com click on shop, images, and cartridges. Select any cartridge click on it and look for the details tap in the middle of the page, click on it and look at the very bottom to see the link for the digital handbook, open it and save it to your hard drive for easy reference.

Sharing Cut Files

A cut file is basically a project that someone has already created and laid out on their Cricut. They then saved the file onto their blog or in the Craft Room. What this does is it saves you from recreating the wheel so to speak.

If you see a project you like you can save the file onto your computer. Then go to the Craft Room and import that file. You can then make the same cuts without having to figure out how to lay everything out. The images are already sized and laid out for you.

The advantage of this is you can save yourself a lot of time by using layouts that others have already done.

But here's the tricky part, you must already own the cartridges the images are from. You can't make the cuts if you don't own the cartridges the images originated from.

You can also save your own projects and share them in the Craft Room for others to use.

When you see a cute project on Pinterest or on a craft blog you might want to ask if the cut file is available and if so, what cartridges it uses.

Organization

If you're like most crafters, including me, you'll eventually become overrun with craft "stuff". You'll have paper stacks, vinyl rolls and other material that you're planning to use someday spread all over your craft area.

Your cartridges may be lying around in a pile and you have to spend twenty minutes searching every time you need a specific overlay or booklet.

Eventually this creates such a feeling of chaos and frustration that you dread going into your craft room or crafting area.

This can all be solved with some organization. It may take you a few hours to get it all in order but it will save you countless hours in the future. You'll no longer feel depressed every time you look at your crafting space.

Craft stores will often have storage containers especially made for certain types of crafts. But you may want to start at your local chain stores. They often have craft and office supply departments where you can find storage units cheaply.

You can find containers where you can sort all your paper into small shelves based on color and type of paper. If you don't like the ones at the craft store then try an office supply store. If you live in an area that's extremely humid; you may want to store your paper in plastic containers.

Another option is to watch for garage sales that say "craft items". Many people spend hundreds of dollars getting set up for a particular craft and then discover they don't have the time or inclination to spend much time actually doing the craft. This can be a bonanza for other crafters.

Photo boxes can be used to keep your booklets and overlays safe and organized.

Some crafters copy their overlays, laminate them and bind them together on rings where they can easily be added or removed.

There are special carrying cases, binders and totes designed just for cartridges. (For cheap Cricut products check out the resource chapter for online deals.)

Computer Files

Along with organizing your physical items; you might want to give some thought to organizing your computer files. It's always good to have a Cricut file to save all your cut files. But you'll eventually want to go a step further. You might want to organize your cut files by project type.

In other words; one for cards, one for scrapbook images, another for signs and one for quilt shapes.

The important thing is to give this a little thought in the beginning. It's easier to set up a computer file system in the beginning and keep everything organized at the start – then to pile everything into one file and try to sort it all out later.

Travel Tips

You may occasionally want to travel with your Cricut to crafting events. It's good to have a sturdy case or tote to carry your die cutting machine that prevents it from shaking around too much. You also want to have room to bring a few supplies.

Resist the urge to bring everything! If you know what projects you'll be working on once you're there it will make it much easier to pack the right amount of paper or card stock that you'll need. Bring some extra in case of mess ups.

If you're able to connect to your laptop and work in the Craft Room then you won't need to bring all your physical cartridges. But you might want to bring a few in case the Wi-Fi connection is bad and for some reason you are not able to connect.

Remember; do not leave your Cricut in your car for long periods if the temperature is extremely hot or cold. The machine should never be left in the direct sunlight.

Chapter Three - Ending the Blade Blues

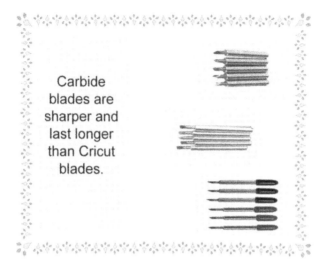

Carbide blades are sharper and last longer than Cricut blades.

Another one of the big problem areas I hear about is with the blades and the housing.

I know, as we've discussed before, we all want to take the machine out of the box and start popping parts on here and there where they look like they fit. We've all done it. Sometimes it even works.

Or sometimes we install things backwards or not tight enough or too tight and end up causing ourselves a lot of unnecessary stress.

Take a few moments to read through the instruction manual. It will be painful, but it won't kill you. I'll be the first to admit that Cricut manuals aren't that great, they leave out a lot of details. However, in general you'll do better reading the instructions then ignoring them and just winging it.

Also, if you do have a problem you can't fix and need to use your warranty; you want to be sure you've followed directions and haven't done anything that would void your warranty.

For an extra safe tip always remember to unplug your machine or at the very least make sure it is turned off when installing or replacing the blade. These cutting blades are sharp and you do need to take common sense precautions. If you have small children make sure they can't access the machine when you're not around.

Installing the Blade

When you first get your machine; you'll need to install the blade housing. Your machine should be set on a stable table that won't shake and has at least two feet of space to load and unload your cutting mat.

Look through the box and make sure you received all the parts. This will include the blade and housing, your power cord to plug the machine in, the USB cord to connect to your computer, and all your manuals and quick start guide. (If you lose your manual you can do a search and find an online version in PDF form and save it on your computer) You should also have some plastic dust covers that pop into your machine to …well…keep the dust out.

Open the front of your machine and take out any cardboard you see. This is placed in the machine to keep everything in place during shipping. You need to remove any cardboard or tape that will keep the parts from moving.

Your blade should already be installed in the housing unit. To double check you will need to push the little button on the top to get the blade to pop out. If the plastic covering is still protecting the tip remove it.

You then need to unscrew the blade holder in the machine so it will swing out. Don't unscrew it so much that the nut completely comes off. Remember "righty tighty, lefty loosey"; in other words, turn the knob to the left to loosen it. Install the blade housing with the arrow facing forward and the blade on the bottom. Then tighten the nut so the blade housing is secure. It shouldn't be wobbly or loose.

Watch out for this newbie mistake when installing your blade housing for the first time. Make sure the arms fit around the first indentation and not the second one closest to the blade. No matter how much you increase the blade depth it will never cut in this position because the blade will never reach the paper.

The blade depth is actually located there on the blade housing (numbers 1 thru 6) as opposed to the other settings that are controlled by the screen and keyboard or by dials. You'll probably want to set the blade depth at 2 or 3 in the beginning. But you will need to adjust this if your cuts are not being made properly or when you use extremely thick material.

Changing the Blade

After a while you'll notice that your cuts are not as clean as they once were. Make sure there is no lint or adhesive glue sticking to the blade. If you have adjusted your settings to make sure the pressure and blade depth is correct for the material you are cutting and that the speed is correct for the size and type of image you selected and nothing has improved, it may be time to replace the blade.

It's estimated that each blade will last for 500 to 1,500 cuts. But that is determined by what material you're cutting. So it's very hard to estimate how long a blade can last.

Before changing the blade always unplug your machine.

You remove the blade housing by unscrewing the nut on the side of the housing until it swings out. Pull the housing out of the machine. Push the button on the housing and very carefully pull the blade out with tweezers or stick it into an old eraser and pull it out. Dispose of it carefully where it can't be picked up or stepped on accidentally. The new blade will usually come with a plastic cover over the sharp edge. Be careful as you remove the plastic tip on the blade for obvious reasons. It's sharp! It's a good idea to place this plastic tip over the old blade before throwing it away.

Then slide the new blade into the housing. It is held in place by a magnet. The magnet will pull the blade into the housing with a snap and hold it in place. You won't need to push it in to get it to stay. You will hear it click when the magnet sucks up the blade.

Then put the housing back into the holder in the machine and screw the nut on the side until the housing is secure.

Deep Cut Blade

You'll want to use the deep cutting blade when cutting thicker material such as vinyl or chip board. It comes with its own housing so you'll replace the entire housing, not just the blade.

Scoring Tip

You may have seen the suggestion that tells you to turn the blade around using the dull end to emboss or score with. I know a lot of people have tried this and liked it but let me tell you what happened to a friend of mine who tried it and wished she hadn't.

Seems the bearings were scratched inside the housing and she had to replace it.

If you don't want to buy a scoring blade at least you have been warned what may happen.

Carbon Steel Blades

There's nothing more frustrating than buying replacement blades that are dull right out of the package. The lack of quality control has caused some Cricuter's to look for alternatives.

It seems there are a number of compatible blades on the market. These other brands make a 45° blade that is compatible with the Cricut regular blade and 60° blade that works like the Cricut deep cut blade. Here are some suggestions.

Gazelle Blades

Roland Blades

Clean Cut Blades

These carbon steel blades may be more expensive but they tend to be sharper and last longer. Just do a search for the brand name and the size you want like this 45° Roland cutting blade to find a variety of price points to choose from.

Cutting Problems

If you've adjusted all your settings and the material is still tearing then you may have to call the Provo Craft service desk to ask for help. There have been some machines sold that have defective housings. If you're unfortunate enough to get a defective machine then you want to be sure and get it back to the company before your warranty has expired.

It's always a good idea to try your machine on several types of material within the first few weeks. This way, if there's a problem you'll find it quickly.

Make sure you **save your receipt**! Provo Craft will not honor your warranty unless you have your receipt.

I've talked to some crafters who prefer to buy their machines through Amazon because they feel their return policy is better than buying directly from Provo Craft.

Chapter Four - Cutting Mat Miracles

Mats are a problem area for many Cricut users. They often feel like Goldilocks – this mat is too sticky and this mat is not sticky enough. Finding the "just right" mat can be tricky. In this chapter we will discuss some ways of caring for your mats and making them last as long as possible.

Cutting mats come in various sizes. The smaller ones are 12 x 6, 12 x 8.5 and 12 x 12. The largest one is 12 x 24. The mats have a sticky surface so they hold your paper in place while it is cut.

The mats were not designed to last for the life of your machine. You will need to replace them periodically. However, there are ways to extend the life of your mat which we'll be talking about in this chapter.

Be sure you press the paper down firmly on the mat. This is especially helpful if your mat has just started losing its stickiness. Make sure the paper is firmly stuck to the mat before loading the mat into the machine.

One way to extend the life of your mat is to switch back and forth occasionally from the landscape to portrait mode. This means your cuts will be spread more evenly over the mat. Otherwise the mat will soon start to show wear and tear from the same area being used the most.

I know the mats are supposed to be directional meaning you load it with the arrow pointing toward the machine, but I have known some to say they alternate loading the mat from the bottom to extend the life, so the same area is not always being cut.

One complaint I here from Cricut users is their new mats sometimes arrive too sticky. This is a rather easy fix. Get a clean t-shirt or some other clean material and as lint free as possible and simply press it on the mat. It should remove the excess stickiness. Then use a lint roller over the mat. You can also use your hands and pat the mat, the oil from your hands will reduce the tackiness.

Matter of fact, I use a lint roller on my mat after every few cuts. A little lint stuck to the mat or to the blade can ruin your cut and rip the paper.

If your mat has lost its stickiness there are numerous ways to "resticky" it. However, it is important to note that if your machine is under warranty that adding adhesive to the mat can void the warranty. So consider your options before deciding to do this until your warranty time is over. Buying a new mat might be a better option.

Some people use baby wipes to clean their mats or just simply wash the mat with soap and water. You can use your spatula to scrape any excess paper or gunk off your mat. If you don't have a spatula a credit or gift card will also work.

Cleaning and Resticking Your Mat

After a while your mat will have a variety of gunk stuck to it. One way to clean the mat is with a product called Goo Gone. The first thing you need to do is cover the edges of the mat with blue painter's tape. You don't want any cleaning or adhesive product to be on the part of the mat that goes under the rollers in your machine. This can cause your mat to not move through the machine cleanly and to get gunk on the rollers.

After all the edges are covered with tape; spray the mat with the product. Three or four sprays are sufficient. You don't want to over spray. Then let the mat sit for ten or fifteen minutes.

Then take a small nail brush, a toothbrush will even work, and scrub the mat carefully. The stuff should come off easily. If not, you can spray it again and let the mat sit longer. But most paper remnants and glitter will start to come off. Then get a clean rag and just wipe the mat off.

Next, you'll need a product called Easy Tact. Spray the mat lightly. Again, you don't want to over spray. Follow the directions and only use this product in a well-ventilated area. Let the mat sit for at least fifteen minutes before you use it again. You don't want it to be wet when it goes through your machine. It's not a bad idea to let it sit overnight before using it again. Don't forget to remove the tape from the edges when you're done!

Another product that some users have suggested to restick their mats is Allene's Tack-it glues. With this product you'll need to have a foam brush or sponge and apply a thin layer of the glue to your mat. Add water to the glue – equal parts of glue and water.

Again, be sure it is completely dry before you try to use your mat. It is still important to cover the edges of your mat with tape before your apply any type of glue or adhesive.

I prefer the Easy Tact, myself. But you can try different products and see which works best for you.

Zig Two Way glue is another option. Because it comes out blue; you can be sure you're covering the entire mat since you can see clearly where you've applied the glue.

Instead of applying repositionable glue to the entire mat why not just add it to the back of the card stock or chipboard you're working on. Here's a real time saving tip. Have several mats handy with the whole project laid out, now you can cut out all your designs at once.

Mats that have lost some of their sticking power work well enough with gel pens or markers when all you want to do is draw.

Another option some Cricuter's use is scotch taping their paper to their mat. They tape their paper on all four sides before loading the mat into their machine. Some use regular tape and others use double sided tape or painters tape. If this works for you it can save you from having to restick your mats.

Remember; when you're using any adhesive product on your mat -- let it completely dry before you try running the mat through the machine. Avoid getting adhesive on the sides of the mat where it can get onto the rollers.

Problems Loading Mat

If you have trouble loading the mat into your machine I find that just unloading and reloading sometimes helps. Make sure you are loading the mat with the arrows pointing the right direction. However, I know some crafters who have had luck with loading the mat from a different direction, not the way the arrow was pointing, and corrected the problem that way. So try it from a different direction and see if that helps.

Sometimes a slight push down and forward, giving it a gentle nudge will help the mat load.

Make sure the mat is under the plastic guides and not too far to the left or the right. It needs to go into the machine completely straight.

Have you ever tried loading the mat and all it does is vibrate against the rollers or you see the rollers moving but they don't grab the mat? Try reducing the pressure for a simple fix.

Also, make sure the mat is not curled in anyway. This can sometimes happen when the mat is shipped to you. Try a new mat and see if you still have the same problem.

The life of your mat is affected by how many cuts you make and how deep. Once the mat has enough cuts to make it rough feeling you may start having trouble with your paper tearing. In that case, it's time to replace the mat or make a new one! (See the video tutorial on making your own mats.)

Make sure all your images are in the cut zone. The Cricut does not cut the full size of the mat. (Unless you know this paper saving tip found in the video tutorial section.) There is a no cut zone around the edges and it can cause a problem if your images are running over into that border area.

One final tip for all you frugal folks out there, here's how to get two for the price of one. Have you ever considered cutting a larger mat to make two smaller ones? One 12 x 24 mat suddenly becomes two 12 x 12 mats and a 12 x 12 mat yields two 6 x 12 mats.

Chapter Five - Working With Gel Pens and Markers

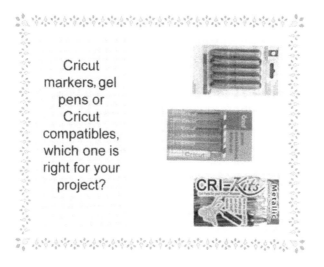

Cricut markers, gel pens or Cricut compatibles, which one is right for your project?

Another great option you have with your Cricut machine is using markers to create images as opposed to cutting the images out. This gives you a multitude of options for card making. I like to use the markers to outline before I make cuts. This makes the cut images stand out more. It's just another creative way to use your Cricut.

The pens can also add designs within the cuts. For example, a Mickey Mouse image might cut out the shape of Mickey, but the pen will draw the details inside the shape such as his eyes and clothing.

With this design option you can turn any image into custom stickers or make coloring books with all your kid's favorite characters.

Pens are also good for shading or highlighting cuts.

You'll have to remove the blade housing and replace it with a marker or a pen holder. I always put a piece of scrap paper under the pen so I don't write on my mat or paper accidentally.

You can NOT move the carriage at all when you switch out the pen and blade. If you do, then the cut and the outline the pen made will not match. To match exactly you need to be sure you don't move the carriage at all.

Select the image you want to draw and hit the cut button, the marker will draw the design. If you want to cut it out, press the load paper button and the carriage will return to the starting point. Never unload the mat because your images will not line up. Remove the marker and install the blade housing. (I know I told you to always turn off your machine when working with the blade, but this is the exception. If you turn off the machine it will "forget" the last instruction, so **don't turn it off, just be careful.**) Now press the repeat last key and the cut button and watch the magic happen.

You can purchase markers and gel pens from Provo Craft. There are also other compatible pens and markers from other manufacturers. For the best quality look for pens that are acid free, archival safe, do not bleed or fade and are waterproof.

Follow the settings given on the maker. You may have to increase the pressure and speed when you are done drawing and want to cut out the image.

Markers will usually provide a darker, wider line. Gel pens are better for thinner, lighter lines. Which to use will depend on the end result you desire for your project.

You can also lower the pressure to obtain thinner lines. The harder the pen is pressing down the darker and wider the line will be. But don't increase the pressure too much or it will ruin the tip of the pen.

Not only can you find a variety of different colors; there are also metallic colors such as bronze, gold and silver. These can add a completely different look to cards. You can also get glitter pens too.

Another use for the markers is to use them to preview how a cut will look on vinyl. This can help you choose the best font or size for your project. Just try different options with the pens until you find the one you like best. Then make your cuts.

Chapter Six - Used Cricuts the Good the Bad and the Ugly

A popular way to save money on Cricut machines is buy them used. That can be an especially good idea if you're in a crafting club or group and know who you're buying from. Crafters often want to upgrade and will sell their old machines cheaply.

Also, we know there are always people who go "gung-ho" into a hobby and buy everything available. A few months later they're bored and want to move on to something else. One of the big advantages of buying a used machine is that you may also get extra supplies or cartridges.

You can sometimes find used machines on eBay and Amazon. The obvious downside to this is you have no way of knowing if the machine works – or at least works well. It can be a hassle to try and get your money back. If the seller has a rating it can give you some idea if they are reputable in their dealings.

Another option is Craigslist. This does have the advantage of being a local seller. You can visit the seller and see how the machine works before you buy.

When purchasing a used machine ask to see it cut several types of material. A machine that works great on paper might have problems cutting card stock. You might want to bring some material with you in case the seller doesn't have card stock or vinyl so you can do test cuts yourself.

If you're buying cartridges with the machine you should always ask if the cartridges have been linked. If they have then you'll only be able to use the cartridges when you have them physically loaded into your machine, they will still cut but you won't be able to relink them in the Craft Room or the Gypsy.

Ask the seller if they bought the machine new and how long they've had it. Also, ask why they're selling. Many times it's just because they decided they don't have time for crafting or don't enjoy scrapbooking as much as they thought they would. But it could be they're having a lot of problems with the machine. Of course, they won't often admit this to you. But sometimes you can tell a lot simply by their hesitation when you ask the question.

Garage sales and thrift stores are another possible way to find used machines. Again, the advantage is they often come with several cartridges included and you get to test the machine to see if it is still working properly.

Buying a used machine can be a great bargain, but as the saying goes, "buyer beware". Try to get as much information as you can before you make your purchase. Ask about customer satisfaction and if there is a money back guarantee.

Chapter Seven - Favorite Adhesives Paper and Tools

Having the right supplies makes your job easier. Use acid netural and archival safe products for good results.

A big question with new scrapbookers and crafters is; what is the best adhesive to use.

I admit to being personally fond of glue dots. You can find them online and in most craft stores. They're a permanent adhesive and maintain their bond on many types of material. They're easy to use and I don't worry about getting too much glue squeezed out of a bottle accidentally. They're also less messy than many other kinds of glue and can be used for small pieces of projects. Pop-up dots add dimension to any project, they just peel and stick to everything from paper to wood, fabric, plastic and even metal.

Many crafters swear by their double sided adhesive tape applied with a gun or glider. The Scotch Applicator Gun is one of the best choices. It uses an acid neutral tape that will not damage family photos or yellow any paper. The Scotch ATG applicator can hold a roll of 1/4 inch or 1/2 inch tape, just right for most Cricut crafts.

It releases the tape in an accurate and easy to use manner. It removes and stores the liner as it releases the tape. The roll of tape is very large and lasts a long time. I find this to be well worth the money and usually look for deals on several rolls of refill tape to stock up. There are cheaper versions but I haven't found one that works as well.

For acid-free and archival safe glue, the Zig family of glue pens is a popular choice. The fine tip pen is perfect for applying glue to your intricate designs. Or you can use the wide mouth roller for bigger jobs. Depending on how you apply it, this glue is permanent or repositionable.

Zip Dry Paper Glue is not just for paper but also works with all kinds of embellishments like glitter, beads and metal. What's really nice is it doesn't leave any sticky residue on your finger when you wipe it off, if you make a mistake or change your mind.

Xyron adhesives seem to be popular with crafters and come in a whole line of products; their sticker maker is on my wish list.

I enjoy the American Crafts card stock. The color goes all the way through which means you don't end up with the white core on layered projects.

Some card stocks I've tried are simply too fibrous and don't cut well and often leave a big mess behind.

When trying to cut thin paper it's often a good idea to tape around the edges. This seems to keep it from slipping. Personally, I find really thin paper some of the hardest to cut without tearing.

I have also had good luck the Bazzil and Recollections brands. They can be found at most craft stores or online.

If you're looking for designer paper with more options you may want to try K and Company Designer, but they are a bit pricey.

Remember if you're cutting thicker card stock you may need to use the multi cut function. This means the cutting blade will go over the cut up to four times to make sure it's cutting all the way through.

I have a teacher friend who has tried to use the cheap construction paper she's supplied at her school. It usually rips and sticks badly to the mat. Slowing the speed down and using an old mat helps some.

One type of paper I've heard many complaints about is the single sheet paper and card stock at Hobby Lobby. Many users seem to have a problem with this brand.

Card stock: I personally find 65 lb. card stock to work the best. Thinner stock doesn't handle intricate cuts as well and thicker wears out my blades too quickly.

Adhesive backed craft vinyl is another material I like to use. It's more expensive than buying regular vinyl but it's easier to use since the adhesive is already added. It usually provides a smoother surface than risking lumps of glue when you attach the vinyl.

When working with vinyl some prefer the KISS Cut method where you just cut thru the vinyl leaving the backing intact, rather than cutting all the way thru.

Accessories You Might Want to Add:

When I first purchased my machine I also added the Cricut tool kit. I have to say I've never regretted this purchase. It contains seven tools and I use them all. The seven pieces include a small pair of scissors which I use on intricate designs, a craft knife that is perfect for removing projects from the mat, a hook tool great for vinyl, a scoop, a bone folder for scoring paper, a ruler and a scarper. They come in a plastic bag for easy storage.

I've recently added a very sharp pair of needle nose scissors and a few old dental picks to my arsenal. I just lift and snip anything that doesn't cut all the way, works like a charm. (My hook tool broke and rather than buying another kit I just asked my dentist to save any picks he was discarding, free is always good.)

Another tool I use a lot is the spatula. I find this to be the most practical for removing projects from the mat without tearing them.

I keep a lint roller to roll across the mat to pick up small pieces of fiber that stick to the mat.

Tweezers come in handy for just about everything.

I always keep at least one deep cut blade on hand for when I'm cutting thicker card stock. This keeps me from wearing out my regular blade as quickly.

It's never a bad idea to have extra mats on hand. If you don't have time to restick your mat and have a late night project to finish; having that extra mat can save a lot of stress.

Blue painters tape is always a good supply for any craft room. It can be used to cover mats if you spray them with adhesive. It can also be used to hold paper to a mat if the mat has lost all of it stickiness.

Provo Craft comes up with new products from time to time but before I buy anything I like to wait until

I've heard a few comments from friends or read reviews in Cricut forums before I purchase. It's always good to know if others had good luck with the product before spending money on it.

Chapter Eight - Money Saving Tricks

For money savings bargains search for Cricut lot or lots on eBay.

We've already talked about saving money by buying a used Cricut. It can be a great way to get a machine at a drastically reduced price. It might work out fine or it might not. There are always risks with used machines. Refer back to Chapter Six for the best places and ways to buy used machines.

When you first buy your machine; you may be offered a special package deal to purchase tools or cartridges at a reduced rate. This can often be a good way to take advantage of discount pricing. Search for Cricut bundle or bundles.

Another way to save money is by watching for sales at your local hobby stores. If you get on their email list you can often get coupons for 10% - 25% off sales.

Watch for sales online and offline. Hobby stores will often run sales on paper and other materials. Even the Cricut cartridges often go on sale. So always look at the flyers or emails they send you.

If you find a particular brand or type of paper you might want to consider buying in bulk.

A lot of crafting clubs have email lists and share information about the latest sales at hobby stores and online.

Another option is to buy bulk packages with your crafting group and then divide them.

I know some crafters get vinyl from sign shops. They can buy pieces at much lower rates. Some sign shops even give them their scraps for free.

As we talked about in the cartridge chapter; you can save money by sharing or borrowing cartridges from friends.

Garage sales are another way to possibly save money. A friend of mine recently found a Cricut machine at a garage sale for a hundred dollars, doesn't seem like a great deal – but it came with ten cartridges.

Sign up for the Cricut rewards program. When you buy products you'll get points that you can then use to buy other products when they are in stock. All the good deals seem to go fast!

My Favorite Bargain Hunting Tips:

We all know that craft supplies bought at specialty stores can be expensive. Often times you can get the exact same item or a similar substitute at considerable savings if you think like a bargain hunter rather than a crafter. So the next time you're shopping for craft supplies consider these venues and enjoy the savings.

My personal favorite is the good old $.99 store

Clearance, wholesale and discontinued merchandise type stores

Thrift stores and junk shops

Home improvement and hardware stores, office supply stores

Yard sales, flea markets or car boot sales

Charity auctions, rummage sales and bazaars

Reverse auction, penny auctions and white elephant sales

Pennysaver want ads, community bulletin boards and online classified ads

Remember one man's or woman's trash is another's treasure. Oftentimes people don't know the value of their unwanted or unused items, but you do! And if by chance you run across a super bargain, scoop it up, if you can't find a use for it, you can always sell it or trade it.

Tell your family and friends to keep an eye out for craft supplies when they shop and to have your phone number handy when they find a bargain.

Consider group buys. Even higher-priced items can be within your reach if you share the cost with friends. When you pool your resources with other crafters you get more for your money.

Trade or barter. If a friend has an item you'd love to own but you have nothing to trade, think outside the box. Provide a useful service like babysitting, running errands, doing yard work or make a fantastic dessert. Being helpful will do wonders for your friendship not to mention winning you the coveted prize.

Wholesale and lot buys. When looking for deals on eBay make sure to include the words wholesale, lots or lot in your keyword search.

If you are looking of Cricut lots, here is a good place to start.
http://cricutdiecuttingmachine.com/Store/cricut-lots

You can also search by specific category to find wholesale lots.
http://www.ebay.com/sch/allcategories/all-categories

Look at the bottom of each category and you should see wholesale lots, if not click on see more and look for it. When you find the wholesale lots link click on it and you'll be taken to the search page. Use broad terms like crafts, scrap booking, rubber stamps to get the most results. I did a search in the collectibles category clicked on wholesale lots and typed in **junk drawer** and found a ton of cool embellishments.

Or just type in junk drawer jewelry from the eBay home page and sort by lowest price to find all the beads you could ever want to decorate anything on the cheap.

Reuse, repurpose and recycle. The $.99 store is filled with craft supplies that didn't start out as such. It**'s** filled with plastic storage containers that with a little imagination can be turned into cartridge storage totes. Helpful hint -have in mind the storage container you're trying to copy. Search online or visit your craft store and take note of the dimensions and the style. That way when you're at the $.99 store you will know what to look for and how much modification you will have to make to duplicate the expensive storage tote.

Make your own storage pockets for cartridge overlays and booklets that fit into binders by looking for clear plastic sleeves.

Hardware stores carry trays with little compartments for storing nuts and bolts. Look for ones that will hold your cartridges.

Some toolboxes come with inserts or trays that are partitioned off into little compartments. Check to see if the dimensions are the right size for your cartridges. A word to the wise, make sure your hubby has no further use for his toolbox trays BEFORE you grab them. This might be an item you look for at flea markets or yard sales rather than his workshop or garage.

Old fishing tackle boxes are also a source of trays and inserts that may just be the right size. If they don't fit your cartridges consider using them for other embellishments like beads, tags, rhinestones, buttons or charms.

Cropping parties are a great way for like-minded people to meet and have fun. You can share your product recommendations as well as your favorite tips and tricks. Why not suggest or organize a "swap meet" at your next crop. Bring your supplies or completed projects that you are willing to trade or swap with other crafters. Let's say you love making greeting cards or you went wild and created a bunch of scrap booking layouts and another party goer has brought a bunch of stickers she'd like to trade for your completed scrapbook pages, you get the idea.

Chapter Nine - Conquering Craft Room Chaos

Clutter and chaos rob you of your crafting time. Keep your craft space organized with these time saving tips.

There's nothing worse than spending your precious crafting time hunting for supplies, rather than creating beautiful projects. Here are some helpful organizational hints that will keep everything in its place and make it super easy to find.

When space is limited consider using every available surface for storage, like the back of a door, the edge of a shelf, the space under a cabinet above the counter and if you're really desperate for space install an overhead storage system on the ceiling.

If you don't have a craft room but use the kitchen table instead here are some smart suggestions. Keep all your supplies neatly organized in a suitcase on wheels. That way you can easily move and store everything you need in one place.

How about turning a rolling kitchen islands into a portable craft room? The butcher block or stainless steel tops provide an excellent work surface and the drawers or shelves furnish needed storage.

Is the Craftbox on your wish list? This is specialized furniture for crafters that cost about 900 bucks. But I like my money-saving suggestions better. Can you convert a closet into a craft room? What about a used armoire, bookshelf or an old entertainment center, with the addition of a drop-down table all you need is a chair.

Don't throw away those baby food jars, they make great storage containers. To conserve counter space you might try nailing or screwing the lids of the jars on to a board and then attach the board under your cabinets above the counter. Then simply fill the jars and screw them into the lids. All those tiny hard-to-find items will be displayed nicely in the row of jars.

Turntables are not just for records. Use Lazy Susan's to organize items you use routinely instead of throwing them in a drawer. You can build stackable rotating trays and triple your available storage. Tin cans or mason jars fit nicely on the round trays and hold any number of items.

No wasted real estate here. Remember I mentioned the back of the door well this is the perfect place to hang a see-through plastic shoe organizer. It comes with dozens of pockets that are perfect to stuff full of craft supplies. Do a search on the Internet for door pockets or over the door organizer to find dozens of styles to choose from. If you like to sew you can make your own out of fabric. You can organize the items alphabetically or by category or by how often used. Make sure to label each pocket for easy identification.

You can mount a magnetic tool strip or self-adhesive magnetic tape to the edge of a shelf or counter. Any metal tool that you use often will be right at your fingertips.

Another under the counter trick is to install a wooden closet dowel, that's the rod your clothes hang on. Then attach clear plastic pockets to close hangers and fill them up.

Peg boards can be configured in 100 different ways. Customize yours horizontally and vertically to squeeze out every last inch of usable storage space.

String and embroidery floss can be kept from unraveling by wrapping them around clothespins and securing the end.

Any container with a plastic lid like a coffee can or cottage cheese container is a cheap way to keep your yarn and ribbon organized. Just cut a hole in the plastic lid and thread the yarn or ribbon through it pulling out as much as you need each time.

Try to keep rolls of vinyl on hangers or somewhere they can remain rolled up instead of getting squished by having something set on them. This can crinkle the vinyl and increase the odds of it tearing as it goes through the machine.

Templates save time. If you have a favorite greeting card designs and scrapbook layouts that you reuse consider making templates. Create your favorite templates and keep them in a binder or punch a hole in them and keep them on a ring. That way you can flip through them and never be stuck for an idea.

My friend Katina is the most organized crafter in the world. Visit her blog to learn a bunch of great tips and tricks. Her mission is to inspire and help you with all your paper craft projects.
http://www.lovinglifeslittleblessings.com/

Chapter Ten - Turning Ordinary Days into Special Occasions

Bring a smile to someone's face and make their day special with a personalized greeting card just for them.

I'll never forget the look on my husband's face when he met the postman and thumbed through the mail expecting the usual ads and of course a bill or two, when suddenly he came across an envelope with his name on it, written in my handwriting. A puzzled look on his face gave way to a big grin as he read the handcrafted card filled with heartfelt sentiment. That beautiful smile filled his face and a tear welled up in his eye.

My husband is an avid sailor, but the pressures of life and the unexpected demands on his time kept him from enjoying the ocean blue for quite some time.

So I created a card chock full of sailing motifs and filled it with loving sentiment and mailed it to him. Needless to say we spent the next three Saturdays on the old Catamaran out on the ocean enjoying each other's company.

So ladies when designing your card make it as personal as possible by using a theme that's near and dear to his heart for lasting memories he will cherish. Besides expressing your love why not invite him out for a night on the town and you'll pick up the check. Or tell him to expect the best home-cooked meal he has ever had. If you've had a bit of an argument this is the perfect way of saying you're sorry and telling him you've planned a very special evening at home to make it up to him.

If you mail it to your home make sure he picks up the mail or if you send it to his office, write "personal to be opened by addressee only" so his secretary will not open it. Have fun with this tip, we certainly did.

Now if you have children create a custom card just for them. Fill it with praise, appreciation and recognition. Kids love getting mail addressed to them. They don't have to win the Nobel Prize for you to commend them. Any simple event will do. Thank them for their help around the house, doing better at school, or if discipline was administered tell them you have confidence in them that they won't repeat the offense. Make sure to tell them about the special day you have planned especially for them. Why not give this tip a try too.

One final thought I never knew how much my mother valued the cards I sent her till she died. I found a stack of cards I sent her over the years, she kept everyone. Had I known that, I would've sent her many more. So friends get busy making those cards.

Chapter Eleven - Warranty Warning

Provo Craft has decided to discontinue the Cricut Imagine, Cake and Create machines, as well as the Gypsy and the Design Studio software. The Gypsy and Design Studio have not been updated since April of 2013. Repair services are still offered on the Gypsy.

These discontinued machines can still be purchased from retailers while supplies last. Technical support will still be provided and the one-year warranty will be honored on registered machines.

Since these machines have been discontinued, knowing that may influence your buying decision, as support may vanish at any time.

Since the Cricut Cake machine has been discontinued some of you may decide to cut edible material with another machine. Please take note you'll void the warranty if you cut any material the machine was not designed to cut. Not to mention the cross-contamination meaning you'll have paper fibers in your frosting sheets and gum paste on your card stock.

Any do it yourself repairs should only be attempted on machines with expired warranties.

Chapter Twelve - DIY Repairs and Resources

For cheat sheets, a gigantic cutting guide and the best Cricut deals online, visit these handy dandy resources.

The number one reason you have to buy a new Cricut machine is when it stops cutting. Well let's see if we can change that with these Cricut hacks! Below you will find common cutting problems and some do it yourself repair techniques. Remember only try these repairs once your machine is out of warranty.

If the blade housing is not going up and down like it should the simplest repair is to check to see if anything has jammed it and clear out any debris. The next step is to remove the plastic housing and give the coils a little squirt of WD40. Make sure to wipe off any excess that may dip off and reassemble the plastic cover.

The next simple fix when the blade housing is binding, drags across the paper or cuts thru your images is to remove the cover and examine the leaf springs to see if they are bent out of shape. Check the upper and lower springs to make sure they are even and flat not bent or twisted to one side. Give them a pinch to straighten them out.

This next repair involves the wiring. Remove the plastic cover on the carriage car and check to see if any of the red, yellow or black wires connected to the solenoid have come loose and need to be screwed down again. These tiny wires are delicate and the connections can easily come apart. You may also have to replace any broken wires and resolder them using a soldering gun. For complete step by step repair instructions see the video tutorial chapter.

Rebooting Your Machine

Seems the stock answer from customer support is do a hard reset when anything goes wrong with your machine, so I have included the instructions here.

Make sure the machine is off with no cartridge loaded. Turn all three dials down to the lowest settings. Gently move the blade assembly all the way to the left by pulling on the carriage. Look inside the machine in the back for a red button; hold it down for a good five seconds. Now roll the dials up and down several times. Finally press the cut button and turn the Cricut off and let it rest for twenty minutes which should clear the memory and restore the functionality of the die cutter.

For Cricut Expression 2 users watch the videos to reset and recalibrate your cutter.
http://www.Cricut.com/home/support/video-faqs

Handy Dandy Cutting Guide

Look what you can cut	Blade	Pressure	Speed	Multi-Cut
Card Stock	5	5	2	1
Chipboard	*6	5	3	2
Contact Paper	3	3	3	N/A
Fabric	6	5	4	1
Heavy Card Stock	*6	5	2	2
Magnet	*6	3	5	4
Stamp	*4	4	3	1
Stencil	6	5	3	2
Thin Plastic	6	5	4	N/A
Transparancy	3	4	3	N/A
Vellium	4	3	3	N/A
Vinyl	*4	3	4	1

* Indicates using deep cut blade

For a gigantic cutting guide filled with over 500 settings for different kinds of material you can cut with your Cricut machine, visit my friend Megan at http://www.aboverubiesstudio.com/the-cricut-cutting-guide/

Have you seen the Cricut Whispers? These cheat sheets are a handy resource you keep right at your fingertips. Just flip thru the pages to find the answers to common Cricut problems.

http://caramiller.com/if-i-made-the-whispers-whispers-to-go-would-that-make-it-easier-for-you/

Shop and save on cheap Cricut supplies, always in stock and ready to ship.
http://cricutdiecuttingmachine.com

Chapter Thirteen - How to Video Tutorials

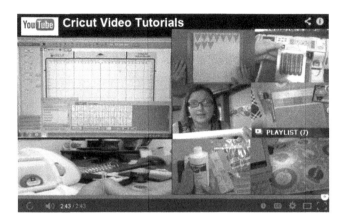

Cricut Markers

Michelle shows you how easy it is to use the Cricut markers to outline your image before cutting it.

http://www.youtube.com/watch?v=wAfaCxHHEG4

Cricut Mats

The first part of the video shows you how to re-stick your mat, but in the last part she explains how to make your own Cricut mats out of cheap table placemats.

http://www.youtube.com/watch?v=tTajr-dCebM

Cutting Fabric

I like this video because it teaches you two ways to cut fabric so you can see which one you like best.

http://www.youtube.com/watch?v=jeblAO4aKbw

Saving Paper

This guy takes paper saving to a whole new level. You will learn how to squeeze in more shapes and make every cut count.

http://www.youtube.com/watch/?v=XAxU9RcfhA0

Favorite Products

Mel recommends some products she uses with her Cricut machine.

http://www.youtube.com/watch?v=85muL-dloIs

How to Repair Your Cricut Machine

Has your machine stopped cutting? If your warranty has expired you have two choices, you can either buy a new machine or fix the one you have. Watch and see how easy it is to fix one of the most common problems Cricut machines have.

http://www.youtube.com/watch?v=n7LJnfPdd08

Cheap Vinyl

Have you seen Cricut vinyl at the $.99 store? Look in the kitchen aisle for roles of shelf liner or contact paper. This is not re-positional vinyl that you would use for wall art. It's just a cheap alternative to have fun with.

http://www.youtube.com/watch?v=vEKwwjryGQY

Cricut Craft Room for Beginners

I chose this video because she shares her fears about being new to the Cricut machine and having to learn even more using the software, so all you newbies take heart, if she can do it, you can too.

http://www.youtube.com/watch?v=8eI6qk9Iy38

Engraving Metal with the Cricut

Here is how to engrave on thin metal with your cutter. Bosskut the makers of the Gazelle die cutter makes an engraving blade compatible with Cricut machines.

http://www.youtube.com/watch?v=nxM_epJW80w

Nail Art

Create beautiful nails with this technique. Have you considered using your Cricut machine to cut vinyl images for fantastic nail art? Since nail polish comes in and endless variety of colors you can mix and match it with vinyl to come up with stunning designs. There are a ton of nail art videos to watch on YouTube and get ideas from. You're only limited by your imagination, so have fun with this tip.

Chapter Fourteen - FAQs

Here are some of the most frequently asked question and answers among Cricut users:

Is there any software I can use that will allow me to use my own designs? Currently no 3rd party software is compatible with Cricut. This wasn't always the case in the past and has made some unhappy Cricut users.

Provo Craft has considered this option but at this time has not offered alternative software to create custom designs. You can still manipulate designs by welding, kerning, flipping, rotating, grouping and shadowing your images. If you are unsure how to do this; visit Pinterest and see some of the designs that other Cricut users have created. They may even let you use their cut files of the designs. Or visit YouTube and watch the helpful tutorials other crafters have posted.

What types of material will a Cricut cut? Your Cricut will cut paper of various thicknesses. It will also cut card stock, vinyl, cardboard and cloth. But for each material you will need to adjust your settings. You may need to use the multi cut function for thicker material. Also, it's a good idea to switch to your deep cut blade for thicker material. (For a quick cutting chart and to learn what other stuff you can cut with your machine see the resource chapter.)

What is a Crop? This is just a get together for Cricut users and scrapbookers.

Can I cut fabric with my Cricut? You can, but it does require some preparation. The best way is to stiffen the material someway so it doesn't slip or slide while it's being cut. You may also need to tape or add extra glue to also assure the material doesn't move. It's best to only cut simple images; not intricate cuts. You'll need to clean your mat and blade carefully after cutting fabric. You'll want to try several ways to stiffen the material and see which one works best for you. Heat n Bond fusible webbing works well.

Does is cost to join the Craft Room? No, this is provided by the Provo Craft company and there is no cost to join.

How can I learn how to use the Craft Room? The CCR has provided many video tutorials to help get you started. You can find them here: https://www.youtube.com/watch?v=5F2kyXwOADg&feature=share&list=PLPvqhFCBvwhsj5G1w-6iHEeZyFAxawJbk

Where can I go to get help with my Cricut? Your first option is the customer service desk at Provo Craft. You can email them or call them. You are usually more likely to get help with a phone call. But the hold times can be long and some customer service representatives are more knowledgeable and helpful than others. Monday - Friday 7 a.m. - 6 p.m. (MST)

Toll free support: 877-727-4288 Fax: 801-794-9001 email: support@Cricut.com

You can find lots of information in this forum as well as ask your own questions. There is even a sub-forum for teachers who use the Cricut for educational purposes. http://www.Cricut.com/forum

There are also other forums for Cricut users that you can find by typing "Cricut forums" in your search engine.

Many blogs are dedicated to helping crafters in many areas; including Cricut information. Just type "Cricut blogs" into your search engine and see what you can find.

There are also Facebook and Yahoo groups dedicated to Cricut users. You can also find many Pinterest pages that show off different project ideas.

What is a Gypsy? The Gypsy is a portable handheld design studio that works with your Cricut. It would be out of the scope of this book to explain the benefits of working with the Gypsy. I may tackle that in my next book.

I'm having trouble using the Craft Room with my Mac? Sadly, you're not alone. Provo Craft has supposedly worked out the issue regarding the security settings. It seems to happen most if Mac users have updated to Maverick on their Mac.

Can I have more than one computer authorized on my Craft Room account? Many people like to have their desktop and their laptop authorized for use in the Craft Room. This shouldn't be a problem since the Craft Room claims they allow two computers for each account. However, many users complain that they have to call customer service and unauthorize a computer every time they switch. This should not be the case; but apparently it is -- at least for some users.

What types of projects can you create with a Cricut machine? The sky is the limit. Many people, like me, originally bought it for scrapbooking projects. We wanted to be able to cut out a multitude of shapes and designs.

But after owning the machine for a while I began to play around with many other creative projects. I'm only going to mention a few to get your own creative juices flowing.

Besides scrapbooking, I think making your own greetings cards has got to be one of the most popular things to create. I love doing layered cards.

I haven't tried my hand at designing and cutting out my own rubber stamps, but I know others who have saved a bunch of money with this option.

You can also use designs from your Cricut to make stencils for t-shirts. There is even iron on heat transfer vinyl for clothes and home decor items like pillows and placemats. Or make your own appliques and apply them to fabric.

I've attached vinyl letters to canister sets, stem ware, picture frames, mirrors and wide variety of kid's toys. You can purchase old children's furniture at flea markets or garage sales and give them new life by painting them and then attaching cute vinyl designs.

Adorable paper dolls with a wide assortment of clothes can be made with the Cricut. These are a great low cost gift idea.

Doll clothes can even be made if you know how to cut fabric. Cutting fabric isn't the easiest thing to do on the Cricut but with a little practice and patience you'll be a tailor in no time. Remember to stiffen the fabric so it runs through the machine properly.

Speaking of fabric; quilters have recently fallen in love with the Cricut. They can cut many quilting shapes with the Cricut in a short amount of time. These can then be sewn together to make amazing quilt patterns.

Magnets are another fun project. You'll probably need your deep cut blade to cut magnet material. You can even create your own refrigerator magnets for your club or business. Or just for fun and profit.

Glass etching and engraving metal is also possible using designs from your Cricut.

Though most people use their cutters for their own personal projects – some users have created their own business selling crafts they make with their machine.

You can set up a booth at a craft fair or swap meet and personalize objects right there while customers wait.

Another option is to set-up your own website to sell your crafts. If you don't want the hassle of your own site – Etsy.com or eBay is a great place to sell craft items without having to create your own website.

Chapter Fifteen - Your Opinion Matters

I had fun writing this Cricut Tips book and I feel it's a helpful, time-saving guide for Cricut users, but that's my humble opinion. What's yours?

Can you please take a minute and leave your feedback. I promise to read every review you post on Amazon. I really appreciate your help, thanks again.

About The Author

I'm all about doing things the easy way, after all crafting should be fun and easy because when it's not it's too much like work. So I got in the habit of looking for quick solutions to all those annoying problems I had, trying to figure out how to get the little bug to make all those fantastic cuts, since that was the reason I forked over my hard-earned money and bought the silly machine.

I wrote all the tips down and when I couldn't find a solution I experimented until I invented my own problem-solving technique.

You've heard that necessity is the mother of invention. Well just ask my husband. He's absolutely amazed at the home repairs I have pulled off using duct tape and a little cardboard, but I digress.

So I got to thinking if these tips, tricks and troubleshooting solutions have helped me, maybe they will help other Cricuter's. If you've seen the forums you know Cricut crafters are generous, love to share and are more than willing to help, ergo the reason I wrote this handy guide.

If I can make it a little easier for you to have fun with your die cut machine that would really make my day.

Have you found any of these tips useful? If so please help me get the word out. Mention this Cricut Tips book on your blog, tweet about it or post your comments on your Facebook page.

Thanks for your help and happy crafting!

Maryann Gillespie